BORNO
■
Maiduguri

Yola
■

Nigeria

Africa

TUNISIA

W.SAHARA

MOROCCO

ALGERIA

LIBYA

EGYPT

MAURITANIA

MALI

NIGER

CHAD

S U D A N

DJIBOUTI

SENEGAL

GAMBIA

L.Chad

GUINEA BISSAU

GUINEA

NIGERIA

Benue

ETHIOPIA

SOMALI REP.

SIERRA
LEONE

IVORY
COAST

GHANA

Niger

CENTRAL
AFRICAN EMPIRE

Nile

LIBERIA

TOGO

BENIN

CAMEROUN

UGANDA

KENYA

EQ.GUINEA

GABON

CONGO

Congo

Z A I R E

RWANDA

BURUNDI

L.Victoria

TANZANIA

ANGOLA

Zambezi

ZAMBIA

MALAWI

MADAGASCAR

MOZAMBIQUE

NAMIBIA

ZIMBABWE

BOTSWANA

SWAZILAND

SOUTH
AFRICA

LESOTHO

Kayodé
and his village
in Nigeria

Written and illustrated by
Carol Barker

Oxford University Press

Oxford New York Toronto Melbourne

ACKNOWLEDGEMENTS

To John Picton, Department of Africa, School of Oriental and African Studies; formerly
Department of Ethnography, British Museum. Also to Philip Allison, formerly with the Federal
Department of Antiquities, Nigeria. And to Dr E. McClelland; Dr Isaac Abayomi, Faculty of
Health & Science, University of Ife; Dr Anne Bamisaiye, Institute of Child Health, University of
Lagos. Also to Oba Jesu Clement Abegunde, King of Aye-Ekan, and to Simeon Abatan
Sangoyomi, Headmaster of St Michael's Catholic Primary School, Ekan-Meje. Also to Mr & Mrs
Oyelola and to Mrs Fashade, and to all the other people who helped me with the research for this
book, and with my visit and journey in Nigeria.

This book is dedicated to:

Thadeus Afolayan, alias Kayode. Also to Chief Afolayan and Aransi, his father and mother. And
to Anthony Fas, who acted as my interpreter and 'guide' at Aye-Ekan.
And to Father Kevin Carroll, who helped me particularly with my research at Aye-Ekan. I thank
them all for helping me to make this book possible.

Preface

Having spent eight years in Africa in the service of the United Nations, including
UNICEF, it is with particular pleasure that I greet the appearance of *Kayode and his village
in Nigeria*. Carol Barker has succeeded in grasping the essence of a Yoruba boy, his daily
life, and the fascinating culture of his people, both in her text and in her superb
illustrations. Through the eyes of the 12-year-old Kayode we learn about his family, his
school, his work on the farm, the trees and flowers and animals which form his
environment, the food he eats, the clothes he wears, the house he lives in, the games he
plays, the myths and traditions of the rich Yoruba culture, its music and ceremonial
dances.

   It is through sensitively written books such as this that children can learn about each
other and can grow to understand each other's differences and the wealth of experiences
which can be shared, if only we can learn to look at life through the eyes of others. The
United Nations Children's Fund welcomes this book, and warmly congratulates Carol
Barker and Oxford University Press for producing it.

Note: Yoruba words are usually accented.
To make things simpler for English
readers, we have omitted all accents,
except for an accent on Kayode on the title
page and cover to help with
pronunciation.

Aida Gindy

Director
UNICEF Office for Europe

Oxford University Press, Walton Street, Oxford OX2 6DP

London Glasgow New York Toronto
Delhi Bombay Calcutta Madras Karachi
Kuala Lumpur Singapore Hong Kong Tokyo
Nairobi Dar es Salaam Cape Town Salisbury
Melbourne Auckland
and associate companies in
Beirut Berlin Ibadan Mexico City Nicosia

© Carol Barker, 1982

Cataloguing in Publication Data

Barker, Carol
Kayode and his village in Nigeria
1. Yorubaland, Nigeria – Social life and customs –
Juvenile literature
I. Title
966.9'00973'2 DT519.9Y/ 80-42418
ISBN 0-19-279737-9

Phototypeset by Tradespools Limited, Frome, Somerset, England
Printed in Hong Kong

A long time ago there lived a great ancestor in the village of Aye-Ekan in Yorubaland, so long ago that that no one can remember his name. He had several wives, and they bore him many sons. These sons grew up and married, and in turn had many sons. One of these sons was called Chief Adetiba, and he had a son called Enijesa Afolayan. He grew up and married six wives. His third wife, named Aransi, bore him five children. The last child was born in 1967, and he is called Kayode (pronounced Ky-o-deh). This means 'This child brings gladness' in the Yoruba language.

Kayode's parents cannot read or write. This is because they were not allowed to attend the Christian school when they were children, because they are Pagans and believe in the Yoruba Gods. So they decided that their youngest son should become a Christian, and they took him to the church to be baptized. Kayode grew up into a healthy boy, and when he was six he went to the Catholic primary school in Aye-Ekan. During the school terms he lived in the main family house at Aye-Ekan, and during the holidays he went to live at the farmhouse, some way outside the village, to work on his father's farm. Kayode is now twelve years old. He told me about himself and his life in the village.

'When the school term finishes in July our father, Chief Afolayan, likes us to go and work on the farm. This year I went with four of my brothers, Julius aged 16, Raphael aged 12½, Bolaji aged 9, and Molade aged 8. We put our clothes in baskets, and carried the baskets on our heads. We walked barefoot along the dirt road through the forest to the village of Ora 4 miles away. Then we caught a bus which went 12 miles to a village called Alariasa. From there we walked through the forest for 1½ miles until we reached my father's farm in the middle of the forest. It was a long and tiring journey.

'In the farmhouse there are three women from the family household who live and work there. Two of them are my father's youngest wives, and the third is the first wife of his eldest son. They fetch the water, prepare the food, and do all the cooking. They look after their husbands, their babies, and all the other children. At harvest time they also help to collect yams and maize.

'When I am on the farm I always carry my wooden catapult (called kanna-kanna in Yoruba). I made it myself with a big sharp knife, and tied a rubber band onto it. I carry a bag full of small stones. I can shoot birds, squirrels, and bush-rats. To shoot a bush-rat, I hide with my brother Julius behind a bush, and wait until the rat comes. Then I shoot my stone to hit the rat and kill it. I carry the rat home, fetch firewood, and make a fire. I burn the hair off the body, clean it, and throw away the rubbish. Then I put some palm-oil, some pepper and salt in a pot and cut the rat into small pieces. I fry the pieces in oil until they are cooked, and keep it until supper time. I roast it and share the cooked meat with all my brothers and sisters. The bush-rat meat tastes quite delicious. If I shoot a squirrel or a bird I cook them too and divide them up amongst my brothers and sisters. You see, the only meat we usually get is from hunting animals in the forest.'

'My eldest brother Andrew is a hunter. He has a gun and shoots and traps small animals. But my father is not a hunter, and we do not eat meat often.

'We work in the fields from Monday to Saturday and make yam heaps with our hoes. I can make fifty yam heaps in a day,' Kayode said proudly.

'During the harvest season my brothers and I dig up yams and bring them in baskets to the farmhouse. We also help to collect the ripe maize. Our father often comes to the farm, and helps us. The work we do depends on which season of the year it is. In the dry season, from November to February, my father clears the ground, burns off the undergrowth and trees, and prepares the heaps. In March he plants yams, maize, cassava, and green vegetables such as okra, peppers, beans, tomatoes, coco-yams, pumpkins, and gourds. When the rains come in April these begin to grow, and so do the weeds. We spend a lot of time just clearing the weeds with our hoes and cutlasses.

'The yams produce one harvest in mid-June, which continues for several months. We harvest maize in June, and then we plant a second crop. We can harvest cassava at any time.

'My father has three plots of land, and plants different crops on each plot every year. This is called rotation. In the first year he plants maize. The second: yams. The third: maize. The fourth: cassava. The fifth: cassava. In the sixth and seventh years nothing is grown, and the ground lies fallow. My father has 4 acres of land here and 2 acres of land at Aye-Ekan. My brothers and I all work hard to help our father grow good crops every year to feed our large family. On the farm I get up at 7.30 am and eat my breakfast of cooked yam with oil. At 8 am I go to the fields and work until 2 pm. Then my father, my brothers, and I return to the farmhouse, where the women have prepared lunch for us. We drink gari (cassava gruel) and we eat eba (fried cassava cakes). We rest after lunch until 4 pm and go back to the fields until 6 pm to do more work. Then we return to the farmhouse and have a rest. We eat supper at 8 pm – pounded yams with vegetable soup. At 9 pm we go to bed, sleeping on rush mats on the floor. We are very tired, and we sleep soundly.'

In the forest I have seen bush-buck, antelope, duikers, wild pigs, and monkeys called ijimere. They live high up in the trees and jump from one tree to another. On our farm we have parrots that we call odidere, and hornbills, which we call atioro. There are many snakes in the forest, but I have not been bitten yet. I like walking through the forest and seeing the birds, animals and butterflies. But I must be very quiet so that they do not run away.'

| Kolajo
Sixth Wife | Maria
Fourth Wife | Christopher | Aransi
Third Wife | KAYODE | Chief
Afolayan |

'I return from the farm at the end of the holidays in August,' Kayode said. 'And then I have one week to prepare for school at the beginning of September. My brothers and I returned from the farm with our father, Andrew the eldest brother, and one of the younger wives. We walked through the forest, got on the bus, and then walked again for the last four miles, all the way to our family house in Aye-Ekan, my native village.'

Elizabeth
First Wife (holding baby)

Cecilia
Second Wife

Afolabi
Fifth Wife (holding baby)

Abiodun
(Kayode's brother)

It was good to see Aransi again, and the other mothers and children. Our family is very large. My father, Chief Afolayan has six wives. His first wife Elizabeth, is the senior wife. She has one son, Andrew. The second wife is called Cecilia. She has six children. The third wife Aransi, my mother, had five children and I am the youngest. The fourth wife Maria has four children, the fifth wife Afolabi has one child, and the sixth wife Kolajo has one son.'

'There were twenty-two children born to my father from all his wives, but six children died when they were babies, from diseases such as chicken pox. But in 1963 a Health Centre was built. Now we have visiting doctors and health workers in the village, and so the children are much healthier.

'Our whole household consists of twenty-five people. Also in the compound there are several grown-up children who are married and have children of their own. My father, Chief Afolayan, has to feed and support them all through the year. We live in two single-storied houses on one side of the compound, and my Uncle Anthony Fas lives with his wife Maria and their eight children, on the other side. The compound is like a large yard, and the family houses are grouped in a square around it. We meet our friends and talk there, and I sit on the porch outside and play a game of arin, with nuts.

'Our family compound is called ode-ede, meaning "the most suitable place". We have forty-four members in our compound, all related to each other. The head of the whole compound is Anthony Adewumi, my father's elder uncle. There are thirteen compounds in Aye-Ekan.

'During the holidays when I am home, I get up at 7 am. I wash my face and brush my teeth with a chewing stick. I greet my father, "Ekaro, Baba" (Good-morning, father). Father replies, "Ajibi?" (Did you wake up well?). I reply, "Adupe" (Thank you). Then I greet my mother, "Ekaro, Mamy". Mother replies, "Ajibi?" and I reply, "Mojio" (I wake well).'

Kayode prostrates himself on the ground in front of his parents, when he greets them. He always does this in front of his elders, as a sign of deep respect. All the boys and men prostrate themselves in front of their elders, while girls and women kneel as a sign of respect.

Kayode continued, 'Then I take my bucket, my brothers and sisters take their buckets, and we all walk to the river one mile away to fetch water for drinking and cooking. Then we collect wood in the forest and bring it home to make a fire for cooking breakfast on.

'On some days we have porridge for breakfast, and on others we eat pounded yam. My brothers and sisters and I take it in turns to prepare yams. First we clean the earth off them. Then we cut them into pieces and put them in water in a pot on the fire. After half an hour the yams are soft. Two of the younger mothers, Maria and Afolabi, put the drained yams in a wooden mortar and pound them with two pestles.

'It is hard work pounding the pestles. Up and down, up and down, bang-bang, bang-bang go the wooden pestles, until the yams are soft and smooth.'

'Meanwhile my mother, Aransi, is making soup with okra, peppers, and red palm-nut oil in a pot on the second cooking fire. When the yams are ready, Maria dishes out a lump of smooth yams in a small bowl for each of us children. Then we all go and sit inside the house on wooden benches, with the okra soup in a large dish in the middle of the table. We each take a handful of pounded yam and dip it into the soup, and eat until the big dish is empty. It is very hot and peppery, my favourite breakfast.'

In the morning I usually go to the kola-nut farm to work with my brothers. After lunch I play arin and football with my friends in the compound. But on market days I help my mother carry her baskets to the market place in Aye-Ekan. She sells cassava flour and groundnuts, and sometimes vegetables to increase the family income. I like the market. There is so much colour and bustle. It is the women who sell things. They sell live cockerels and chickens in baskets, as well as piles of yams, maize, red peppers, okra, kola-nuts, cassava flour in bowls, dried beans, plantains, bananas, and palm-wine. They sell fresh fish, smoked fish, raw meat, cooking pots, jars, plates, lengths of cloth – everything you can imagine.'

In Aye-Ekan the Oba, the King, is the most important person. Each Oba is believed to be descended from Odudua, the god who climbed down from heaven at Ile-Ife to create the world. He had sixteen sons, who all ruled kingdoms in different parts of Yorubaland. Every true Oba is a descendant from one of these sons, and he is the only person who can wear a beaded crown. The Oba of Aye-Ekan is named Oba Clement Abegunde.

Three of six leading Chiefs   Two of the Captain Chiefs   Ifa Divination Priest

He told me about the different groups of people in the village: 'I, the Oba, am the first chief. There are five other leading chiefs, and there are the minor chiefs, who are called captains. They guard the community. Among these captains are Chief Eruku and Chief Enijesa Afolayan (Kayode's father). In the olden days these captains organized the soldiers and cavalry forces and led them in battle. The next group are the religious leaders. In the past they were the chief priests of the Yoruba gods only, but today they are the President of the Roman Catholic church, the chief Imam (leader of the Muslims), and the chief priest of Ifa, the god of divination (meaning fortune-telling), leader of the Pagans. Next in order, come the priests and teachers. After them the traders – businessmen and women. Then come the craftsmen and women – the blacksmiths, tailors, shoemakers, wood-carvers, potters, weavers, and dyers. Finally there are the farmers and their families – the ordinary people.'

Oba Abegunde says: 'It is the people that I represent. I act as their spokesman, and am the chief person responsible for their welfare. I try to keep peace and harmony within the village, and try to improve community life. The Oba before me got the Health Centre built in 1963. Now I am trying to raise funds for a new town hall, and for improved tarred roads. The other things that I would like for our people, with the help of the Kwara State Government, are: first, to get piped water, so people don't have to carry it from the river; second, to have electric light; third, to have our own hospital, and last, to have a secondary school for girls, as there is only one for boys at the moment. If there is a problem in the village, I hold a meeting with the five most important chiefs. I call all the Catholic members together, and we pray in the church with the Reverend Father. Then I call the Imam, the Muslim leader, and tell him about the problem in the village, and ask him and his followers to pray to Allah in his mosque, for help.'

'Then I send for the chief Ifa priest, and ask him to tell the other priests of the Yoruba gods about the problem, and ask them to sacrifice a cock or a he-goat to their Orishas to obtain help. So, all the people from different religions pray together to their different Gods, to ask for help and strength for our people in Aye-Ekan, so that no harm will come to them.'

Ifa is the oracle, and is the most important of the Yoruba gods. His priests are diviners (fortune-tellers), and people come to consult them before taking any important decisions in their lives.

They consult them before marriage, before a child is born, at the birth of a child, before a journey is made, in sickness, and at all the stages of a man's life. A priest of Ifa is called a Babalawo, father of secrets.

At this time Felicia, the wife of Kayode's elder brother Abiodun, had given birth to a baby son. Unlike Kayode, Abiodun was not a Christian. So the Ifa priest was summoned to their house, and Abiodun, Felicia with the baby, and Kayode knelt in front of him. He had to divine which ancestor had been born again in the child, and which god and cult he should follow.

The Ifa priest can choose two methods of divination. He can use his divining chain, or his ikin, a set of sixteen palm nuts. In this case he used the ikin. He passed the sixteen nuts from one hand to the other, and according to how many were left behind, he made marks with his forefinger on his divining board covered in iyerosun powder. Through these techniques the priest can find out the will of God as mediated by Ifa. The marks on the board will tell him which chapter of the poetry of the Ifa oracle he should chant. He chanted the verses of the chapter chosen in this way for Abiodun's baby son. As a result it was clear to Abiodun, his wife, and Kayode that the baby should follow Ifa.

The people in Aye-Ekan make almost everything they need. There is a blacksmith, a cobbler and a carpenter – these are men's jobs. The women make the pottery. Mrs Adeola Babaola is a potter. She says: 'My daughter Taiyewo has been making pots with me since she was a young girl. We make large pots for cooking yams, and others to hold water. We make smaller pots for soup, and very small pots for baby's medicine. We make about four pots a week. When we have moulded the clay pot, we dry it in the sun. Then we fire it outside. We can fire up to ten pots in a day. After firing, we cover them in a varnish made from locust beans to make them shiny black. On market days we take our pots and sell them.'

There is a long tradition of weaving in Yorubaland. Mothers teach their daughters from generation to generation. In Aye-Ekan almost every house has a loom built against the wall. Aransi weaves on a loom in their house. She weaves lengths of cloth about 6 ft long by 2 ft wide. Sometimes the colour is plain and blue. Sometimes the cloth has coloured stripes. Sometimes more complicated patterns are woven into the cloth.

Aransi says: 'First of all I weave cloth for my husband, my children and myself. Then I weave for other people, to make a little extra income. After I weave the lengths of cloth, I take them down the road to the tailor, who makes them into clothes on his sewing machine. I enjoy weaving, but I have to fit it in with my other household duties, so I do not work at it all the time.'

There is also a very fine tradition of wood-carving, done by the men. The craft is handed down from father to son. Joseph Agbana is a wood-carver, living in Aye-Ekan. He says: 'I learnt from my father, Rotimi Agbana of Osi-Ilorin several miles away, a well-known wood-carver himself. I started learning when I was six years old, and worked as his apprentice for eleven years. Then I left home and began work on my own. At first I carved for the Pagans and the secret Ogboni Society. I carved secret society drums, also figures of warriors, hunters, Oshun worshippers, and even the great Epa masks. I was born a Pagan but became converted to Christianity when I was sixteen. One day, Father Kevin Carroll saw my carving, and asked me to do work for the church. Since then I have done many carvings for the Catholic church. I have carved crosses, doors, panels for the fourteen Stations of the Cross, a great altar screen, and figures showing the birth of Jesus. Father Carroll has helped me to adapt my work for the church, and shown me how to use new carving designs and working methods. But I still do traditional carving for the Pagans, and have just completed two more Epa masks. All my carving is done in the traditional Yoruba style. I don't mind whether I carve for Pagans or Christians.'

On the other side of Kayode's family compound lives his Uncle Anthony Fas, a Roman Catholic Catechist (assistant to the priest). He is very wise, and knows all the history of the village. He says: 'For many hundreds of years our people were Pagans and believed in the Yoruba gods and goddesses. But in 1901 the first missionary, an Anglican priest, came to Aye-Ekan, and preached the Christian Gospel to the people. The first convert was a man named Ege, and his brother Oni and their family. They built the first church in 1904. But in these early years, the Pagans hated the Christians and destroyed their church. Then Oni became a Catholic, and many people joined him. From 1923 onwards there was peace between Pagans and Christians. The Anglican church was rebuilt in 1914. Then some people became Muslims, and built a mosque in 1918. The first Roman Catholic church was built in 1924. The Catholics form the largest group today.'

Kayode says: 'I was baptized when I was a baby in the Roman Catholic church of Aye-Ekan. And I have been brought up all my life as a Christian and a Catholic. Nearly all my brothers and sisters are all baptized and Catholics too. My mother, Aransi, is a Pagan, and she is a priestess of the god Obatala. My father is also a Pagan and he worships the god Osanyin, the god of medicine, as he is a native doctor. There is a shrine to Osanyin in our house. I myself do not believe in Osanyin or Obatala. I believe in the one Christian God. I have learned about Christianity at my school and in church. I like to go to church with my brothers and sisters, and it does not worry me that my father and mother do not go to church with us'.

'Every Sunday, when I am living at home. I always go to St Michael's Catholic church for morning service at 9 am with my brothers, sisters, and cousins. My Uncle Anthony Fas takes the service and gives a sermon when the Reverend Father is away. My cousin Francis and I, and two other boys, play the drums in church, and we sing and play in time with the choir. I especially like singing "Our Father":

"Baba wa ti mbe lorun, owo loruko re
owo – owo – owo loruko re,
Ki ijoba re de, Ife tire ni ka se laiye bi nwon ti nse lorun."

"Our Father which art in Heaven, Hallowed be thy name.
Hallow – Hallow – Hallowed be thy name.
Thy Kingdom come, Thy will be done, on earth as it is in heaven."

All the people sing it with the choir. It has a strong rhythm and chorus.'

Kayode's school, St Michael's Catholic Primary School, was started in this very church in 1924 with fifteen pupils and one teacher. In 1944 the present school was built, and has been increasing in size and numbers ever since. Today there are 737 pupils and twenty-five teachers.

Kayode says: 'I was six years old when I started school. I began in Class I and am now in Class VI. I like it at school. I learn arithmetic, social studies, Bible knowledge, health education, general knowledge, English, and Yoruba. My favourite subject is arithmetic. I like making calculations, and I think it will be useful to me when I am older. I have now started my new term at school in Class VI. I returned on September 10th, and this is now my second week back. My new teacher, Mr Alufa, takes our class for social studies.'

As Mr Alufa enters the class, the children stand up. 'Good morning, teacher,' they say. 'Good morning, children,' replies Mr Alufa. The children sit down, and the teacher begins the lesson.

'We Yorubas are one of the largest groups of people in Nigeria. Odudua is the God who climbed down at Ile-Ife to create the world, and he is the first King of Yorubaland. His sons and grandsons founded other kingdoms, and today there must be about fifty Yoruba kings, all claiming descent from Odudua. Of all the Yoruba kings, the king of Oyo was the most powerful and ruled the largest kingdom. But he never ruled the whole of Yorubaland. In addition to Ife and Oyo, some of the other kingdoms are Ijebu-Ode, Ilesha, Owo, and the sixteen kingdoms of Ekiti.

'There were many wars between some of the Yoruba kingdoms in the nineteenth century. The Hausa and Fulani people also marched down from the north to spread their religion, Islam. There was much fighting and bloodshed between us

'The first white people to come to Africa in the sixteenth century were Portuguese traders. They came looking for gold and found it in the area we know as Ghana. Then they came to Nigeria looking for pepper and ivory. Later they bought some of our prisoners as slaves and took them away in ships. Soon this became a regular trade. White people from Britain, America, France, Portugal, Denmark, and Holland started to trade with our kings, and took away many slaves across the oceans to America, Brazil, and small islands in the Caribbean Sea. The descendants of our people there are now called Afro-Americans and Afro-Caribbeans.

'For a long time, Europeans fought among themselves to have the best of the African slave trade. Finally the British became the victors. But gradually the British realized that the slave trade was unjust and uneconomic. In 1808 British ships patrolled our coast to stop slaves being taken away.

'Gradually British trade increased in West Africa, and they gained great influence. In 1852 they recognized Akitoye as the king of Lagos and signed a treaty with him. Nine years later the British forced his son, Dosonmu, to hand over his country to Queen Victoria of England. By the end of the century the British had taken over the western and southern parts of Nigeria as well. Finally in 1914 when the First World War broke out, the British combined the various parts of our country and formed the single colony and Protectorate of Nigeria.'

Kayode stood up. 'Sir, what is a Protectorate?'

'A Protectorate is a country which is protected by a more powerful country for a period of time,' said Mr Alufa. 'Nigeria was a Protectorate for 46 years, and it became independent in 1960. At that time there were three Regions: North, East, and West. In 1976 nineteen states were created'.

'Now, Kayode, what are the names of the states of the Yoruba people?'

Kayode stood up and said, 'The names of the states of we Yoruba people are Kwara State (this state) Oyo State, Ondo State ... um ...'

'And Ogun State!' shouted a boy at the back of the class.

'Correct,' said the teacher. 'And there is also Lagos.' He continued: 'In our country we have four parties, the two biggest are the National Party of Nigeria and the Unity Party of Nigeria. The National Party of Nigeria won the election of 1979, and Alhaji Shehu Shagari became our first executive President.' The teacher concluded: 'You must listen to your radios to keep in touch with political events. If you do that, and read your books properly, you will pass your examination. But if you always look after rodents on the farm, you will not know what is happening in the world.'

Chief Oba-nla Bamgboshe is the chief priest of Shango, god of thunder. He is a native doctor and cures people with herbal medicines. He is also a master bead-worker. He says: 'When I was 17 I made small bead objects for the Oba of Imode. Then I made elaborate high crowns, and other royal regalia for the Obas of Kwara, Oyo, and Ondo States. Sometimes I had to work in secrecy in the Oba's palace, or at my home. I became a master of bead-work and made decorative beaded crowns, ram's-beard whisk handles, Queen's bags, cushions, shoes, and all the Oba's regalia. I worked at this for 40 years, but have now passed on the work to my son Michael. My main duty is as the chief priest of Shango, and leader of the cult. I have my own shrine at home, as do other Shango worshippers. Every year people consult me about the Shango festival. They make animal sacrifices to Shango at home 17 to 21 days before the main festival.'

'I make a sacrifice of a ram and a pig in the compound, facing towards the Shango shrine. We cook the meat and make pounded yam. Then we begin the feast, drink palm wine, and dance. At the main festival, the god Shango possesses me and I have magic powers. I can eat fire, and swallow gunpowder. On that day we have a great procession to the Oba's palace, and after the main sacrifice we have feasting, drinking, and dancing.'

In Aye-Ekan many people, like Chief Bamgboshe and Kayode's father and mother and elder brothers, believe in the traditional Yoruba religion. Yoruba people have believed in their traditional gods for hundreds of years. They believe in many gods and goddesses, some say 600 or more. The Oba Clement Obegunde says that in the olden days people worshipped 420 gods and goddesses in Aye-Ekan, and there used to be 420 festivals each year, one for each god. But nowadays not nearly so many are worshipped. Each person usually worships the god, or goddess, of his father.

These are the main gods worshipped today. First there is the great god known as Olodumare. He is no ordinary god, and has no shrines. He is Olorun, the God of Heaven, the Creator, the King, All-wise, All-knowing, All-seeing, the Judge, Immortal, Holy. Olodumare controls the destinies of mankind. Therefore he can be thought of as the God of Destiny. He is a 'withdrawn' God: the other gods are felt to be closer to men, but he is always in the background.

The general name for the 'lesser' gods, 'the ministers' of Olodumare, is Orisha. The god Obatala makes the human form. He moulds people, and carves them like a wood-carver in the woman's womb before they are born. Hunchbacks or people with deformities are sacred to him, and are marked so that his worship will not be forgotten.

Eshu is the youngest and cleverest of the gods. He delights in trouble-making, and tricks people into offending the gods, so that they must then offer sacrifice to put matters right. Without Eshu the gods would starve. He is also the messenger of the gods, and delivers sacrifices made to them.

Ifa is the god of divination, and helps people to put right the trouble caused by Eshu. Ifa interprets the wishes of Olodumare and the gods to mankind, and prescribes the sacrifices which Eshu carries to him. The Yoruba people regard Ifa as a sure and unfailing source of comfort. Their faith in him is complete.

Ogun is the god of iron and is worshipped by all those who use iron tools. He is the patron of hunters and warriors, and is thus god of war. Blacksmiths, wood-carvers, farmers, leather-workers, barbers, and lorry-drivers all worship him.

Shango is the god of thunder and lightning. He was formerly a king of Oyo, noted for his magical powers. He lives in the sky and sends thunderstones to earth, killing those who offend him or setting their houses afire. People have dug up many stone age axe-heads in the fields, and they believe that these are Shango's thunderbolts. So they put them as symbols for Shango on his shrine. Shango fights with trouble-makers, and those who use bad medicine against others. The priests of Shango are also rain-makers. Every year there are festivals for each of these gods all over Yorubaland.

Oba Abegunde says: 'In Aye-Ekan the most important festival is the Egungun in July or August. In the festival we remember our ancestors. Many kinds of masqueraders (masked dancers) come to the Egungun festival. The first and tallest ones are the Egungun Eleru, the Elder Egungun. They are supernatural, and have magic power. In the olden days they used to persecute witches and kill them, and punish criminals. People are still afraid of them. There are also the small masqueraders, called Parakas, the Children of Egungun. Other masqueraders are the Egungun Alago, dressed in a shroud, and the Trickster Egungun, who have wooden masks. They entertain the people and do magical disappearing acts. The people believe that the ancestor spirits enter into the masqueraders. Anyone who has lost a father or mother prepares food and takes it to the secret Egungun shrine in the bush, and gives it to the sacred spirit of the ancestors.

Oshun is the goddess of the river. Because of her great beauty, Oshun was desired by all the gods, and she took many of them as her husbands. She had many children herself and is famed for giving children to her worshippers. The Oshun river flows through Yorubaland and past the city of Oshogbo where her principal shrine is.

This is the story about it. A long time ago there was an Oba, who lived in a village where there was a bad drought. His people had no water, so he went to look for water and found the river Oshun. As he began to fill his pitcher he heard a woman's voice saying, 'Who are you? What are you doing disturbing my peace?' 'Who are you?' said the Oba. And the voice replied, 'I am Oshun, goddess of the river.' The Oba told her that his village had no water. 'No, you cannot settle here,' said the voice, 'because I do not like noise.'

'But if you move away from this place with your people, I will protect you, and no one will disturb your peace. No war will scatter you.' So the Oba promised that his people would move farther away, and neither make noise nor kill Oshun's children, the fishes of the river. In return Oshun promised to provide them with water and protect them from war. So the Oba came with his people and settled not far from the river, and called the place Oshogbo. Every year since then, the Oba has come for the Festival of Oshun at Oshogbo to renew his pledge. He comes to the river with his chiefs, musicians, and people, and brings offerings to the goddess Oshun. Sacred objects are carried in a calabash by a virgin called Arugba, and she places it near the edge of the river for Oshun in her sacred grove. As the Oba enters the Oshun grove, musicians blow a fanfare on their trumpets, and drummers beat on their drums. Thousands of people come to worship Oshun and greet the Oba. The chief Oshun priestess carries a brass ceremonial sword, and leads the worshippers to the river to fetch the sacred water. The women believe that Oshun will give them children, and protect them for the year. There is music and celebration.

The Egungun Festival lasts for twenty-four days in Aye-Ekan. Now the final day has arrived. Early in the morning the chief priest goes to the Egungun shrine in the bush. He prays and offers kola-nuts to the spirits. Then the masqueraders and all the men in the village come to the shrine with offerings of goats, chickens, and kola-nuts. The chief priest sacrifices the animals and pours their blood on the shrine and on the masqueraders. Then the men collect up the sacrifices, and go back to cook them for the feast. When the food is cooked, all the people gather in the compound outside the Oba's palace and begin the feast.

Then the drummers start drumming, and all the masqueraders come out and dance. They dance around the village, in the market place, and around the street. Groups of drummers, men, women, and children all follow them, dancing and singing. Then the masqueraders go to the Oba, who is sitting with his chiefs outside his palace, and all dance in front of him. At the end of the festival, the chief Egungun priest turns to the crowd and says, 'I give praise to you people, and I pray that you may all live in safety for another year, so that you will be able to see another Egungun Masquerade.'

Kayode says: 'I like dancing in the different festivals. My favourite is the Egungun, because I like watching all the different masqueraders with their masks and coloured costumes. I dance with them, and with the drummers, in a procession to the Oba's palace on the last day. But as I am a Christian I cannot eat the meat of the sacrificed animals, and I cannot sing the praise songs to the Yoruba Gods. But I can dance with them. Christians and Muslims come from miles around to join the Pagans for the Egungun festival, and we all enjoy the dancing and celebration together.

'I like living here in Aye-Ekan now, and helping my father on his farm. But when I grow up I want to be a clerk in the University of Lagos. My mother says she doesn't mind if I don't become a doctor or an engineer, as long as I am happy in my life. But, at the moment, I want to be a clerk. I don't want to be a farmer, because my friends would call me "bush-boy".

'When I am grown up I want to get married, I just want one wife – a nice one! I cannot say how many children I would like, but whatever God wants me to have. Then when I am old, I would like to return here to my native village, and do some farming, and live here on the family compound, just as my ancestors have done from so long ago.'

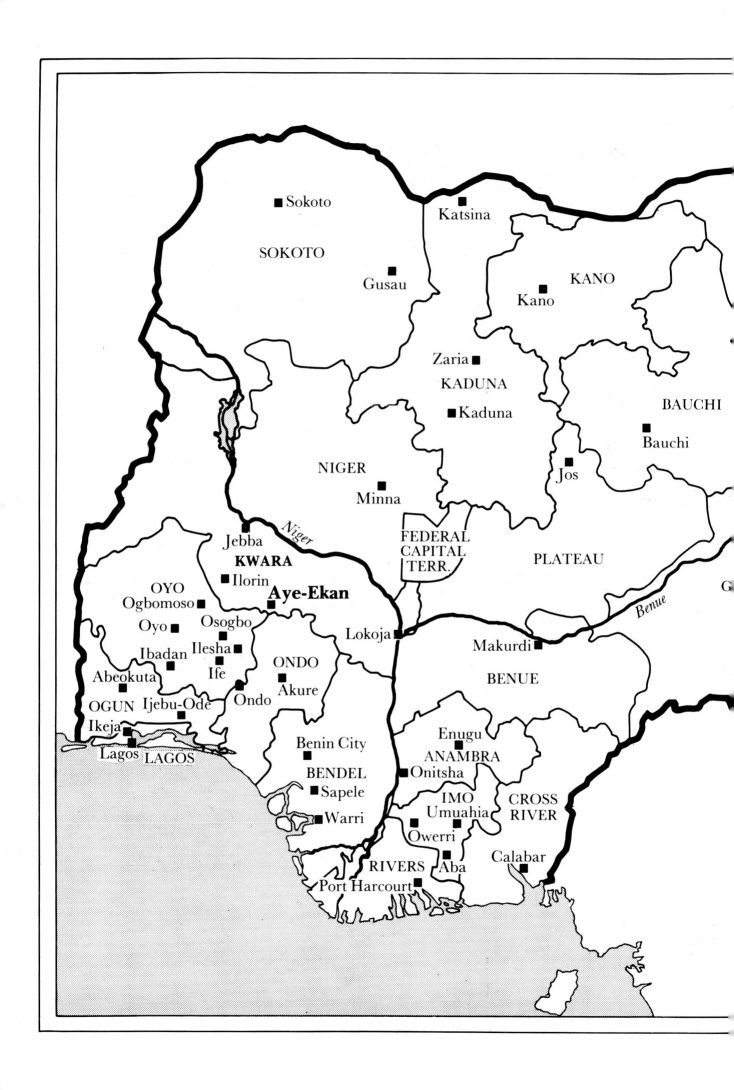